THAT DEEP & STEADY HUM

Also by Mary Ann Larkin

Mary Ann Larkin

That Deep & Steady Hum

*for Henry
who makes us all
laugh...
Mary Ann*

BRP

Broadkill River Press
Milton, Delaware

Published by Broadkill River Press
Printed in the United States of America

ISBN: 978-0-9826030-2-4
Library of Congress Control Number: 2010923238

Acknowledgments follow page 74.

Cover photo of Ben Bulben from Strandhill in County
Sligo, Ireland, by Mary Ann Larkin
Author photo by Patric Pepper

James C. L. Brown,
Publisher
Broadkill River Press
104 Federal Street,
Milton, Delaware 19968
E-mail: the_broadkill_press@earthlink.net

for my poetic family,
those here, those gone

CONTENTS

. . . the never-ending hum . . .
that permeates the universe . . .

from *Longing for the Harmonies:*
Themes and Variations from Modern Physics,

by Frank Wilczek and Betsy Devine

Angell's Toenails

Dianne Cargill's moment came
when Angell, dying, could no longer
paint her toenails luster peach.
Only Dianne noticed the flaking opalescence
where once all had been as satin-smooth
as the color of a sunrise in a fairy tale book.
Angell loved fairy tales and knowing
about Bailey's Beads, how they circled the throat
of the moon every 99 years,
and van Loon's story about eternity.
Dianne knew about jobs and money
and schedules. She went to meetings
and had a palm pilot, into which she entered
Angell's toenails.

And so it was, Saturday at nine:
Angell in her pale-green Japanese kimono
with herons curving round her arms,
now as thin as the birds' necks.
Dianne propped her up
on the wicker chair's paisley pillows,
settled herself on Aunt Ginny's oriental
and poured oil of lavender,
to soften the hard Cleveland water,
into the blue spatterware bowl.
Taking Angell's dwindling feet in her hands,
Dianne stroked the oil
even between Angell's toes,
reawakening her tired blood.

And Angell watched and understood
and gave her feet into Dianne's hands
and spoke of the color peach
and foxes' feet, their song,
and how lavender heals,
and said that when a bird
wears away a mountain
by sharpening his beak
once every thousand years,
one day of eternity passes,
and told Dianne that the touch of flesh
is kin to God.

Dianne Cargill, curls coiled tight
above the steaming water, listened
as she gravely restored to Angell's toes
the mystery of luster peach,
and took from Angell
something Dianne needed
but could not name.
And somewhere between the lavender
and Angell's paper-thin flesh,
between the talk of foxes and eternity,
something came undone in Dianne Cargill,
so that, before continuing on Saturday's rounds,
she sat in her car and wept.

QUIETING THE BABY

Whenever I visited Joanie Costello,
she was next to frantic,
her new baby beet-red and wailing.
I'd wrap the child in my arms and walk,
the baby's face close to mine.
And over and over I'd make
a crooning or a humming sound.
Soon, she'd come to rest.

Joanie Costello would marvel
and beg me for my secret,
but I had little to say.
Only my body knew
how what is deepest in us
calls out what is deepest in another,
the same way the night
pulls the stars from hiding.

ONCE, YOU WILL SAY

we had a yellow house,
and light and air
moved like water
across the yellow porch.
Two white cats dozed
in each other's arms,
then ebbed and flowed
in a long breath
from porch to garden,
where birds sang
out of the green night
of jeweled trees.
And a baby slept.

I tell you all this is true.
And nights when the *zanjero*
opened his gate to flood the gardens,
the moon came down
and swam with the trees.

THOSE DESERT AFTERNOONS

The heat exhaling
a breath just short of burning,
as though across the dusty porch
some somnolent beast padded,
myself half-awake on the plump pillows
of that sheet-draped couch.
The baby asleep inside,
bat-mouthed, bird-boned.
The sun high, almost hidden.
A copper haze. And the stillness.
Only shadows moved.

Evenings, we breathed deeply again.
I showered, sweat-damp
as though from love. The baby
tottered around. The sun
arced away. Coolness coming
as though the rumored beast
had at last inhaled us
into spongy lungs and slept.

All this happened long ago.
I was alone on the porch,
the baby asleep inside.
I can't tell you how it was,
but I gave myself
to those desert afternoons
the same way the baby,
knowing nothing of denial,

fell upon the breast—
with just that amount of birthright
and greed.

Winter Sunporch

Afterwards, we sleep
back into our separate selves,
but our bodies will have none of it.
Shin by shin they lie,
arm over breast
or hand in hand.
The long sweep of them—
toe to thigh to shoulder—
alone together at last.

Now no commotion of limbs,
no moans or spasms,
just themselves, and the sun
lighting the great-armed ferns,
the green throats of the amaryllis,
as the dear abandoned bodies
mingle skin to skin
in a place somewhere
between speech and touch.

How It Was

We had no future,
only sex
and tenderness, its blue flower.
That's what we had
and it wasn't enough
and it was. Bodies
with no future shine bright.
No words
only seed and flesh
cosseted and curved, belly
and skin and bone
on bone. We arced
in and out of ourselves,
earned no reprieve even as
tenderness flowered
in the sated crevices,
the limp arms and lidded eyes
of our exhaustion.
There was a sea.
It was summer,
dawn and noon and night,
a small white room,
ten days, maybe twelve.

THIS IS A SONG

This is a song of grief
for the red wet boy
who didn't come screaming
out of my womb to light,
for the red-haired daughter
who doesn't sulk dreaming
by the plums above the sea.

This is a song of grief
for my belly that never swelled
taut as a blue-veined drum,
for the wild ripe man
with his poems of air
who came too late
with his quick thick seed.

CERTAINTY

God forgive me. The priest made up a bed
in the church and I slept with him there.
Beatrice de Planissoles
Montaillou, France 1292

This holy man takes his woman
straight to God. Is it a flaunting,
a defiance or, perhaps, homage:
  Look, Father, what I bring you,
  alabaster flesh, trembling
  as is seemly when being unveiled
  before the Lord.
Or does he, being a priest,
taste the Divine itself
in Beatrice's sweet crevices,
in pillows of flesh
dimpling to ruby crowns,
even in his fear
before half-moon portals
swelling open—a certainty growing
that the fluted darkness
of Beatrice and the chapel are one.

BAD BOYS

I wanted not to care
  the way they didn't care,
    to see with their hooded eyes,
      climb their laddered torsos
        rib over rib, go
          where I only imagined.

Bad boys,
  float me away
    in your boats of bone and feather,
      dream me a life where
        something matters, or nothing.
          Raven eyes, raven eyes.

CAR RADIO

After we crossed the Tappan Zee
the New York stations came in clear—
jazz and blues, the far-out
and the oldies, the Motown songs
that taught me lust, the folk songs
that lured you to the city—
and we got that feeling
people get, driving all night
with only the headlights and the stars,
that we were young again, and crazy,
and we started singing,
me, belting them out,
knowing only the words,
you, your nuance and sound so fine,
so heartbreakingly fine,
singing Woody Guthrie's old song
"This Land Is Your Land"—
that that's when it happened.
I saw you. I saw you deep,
not the tired guy home from the factory,
not your neurons and muscles,
but I saw the place
where you make your song.

My Guy

In the downstairs kitchen
my guy makes soup,
fusses over his beans.
His Yukon Golds
will be cooked to perfection,
no bite hard or mushy,
but he's worried about the beans.
Beside the simmering soup,
apples on the dryer,
motor oil on the spice shelf,
my guy admires his new crock-pot,
thinks about divine grace.
*

From the upstairs window
he looks out over the alley,
sees angel wings in collard leaves,
rages at the new fence
that severs the line
of yard after yard,
asks me if I believe
the alley cats know
they're going to die.
*

On Saturday night, he watches *Cops*.
Three car chases tonight, he tells me.
When the cops asked them why they ran,
they all said they were scared.
My guy thinks about being scared
in the dark, with all the wrong papers,

maybe a wrong car,
booze and the chase,
sirens and lights,
two guys in cars in the night,
one good, one bad.
It's America, he tells me.

                    *

America, pisspot and dream, he says.
He swears he wouldn't have gone West
with the ancestors, dark-eyed women
who wrung the necks of mad dogs,
men with curled mustaches
who damned sharecroppers,
rode horses thin as wind.
Everyone was mean, and beautiful.

                    *

My guy thinks about America,
death, and love.
No one had enough, he says.
*I'd have gone north to New York,
gotten a room by myself
somewhere in the middle of it all.
I'd have been an American.
You don't need a covered wagon.
You just need to dream, and be lonely.*

KEEPING TIME

Here I loll in the bowl of the world,
someone's finger on the Pole Star
spinning me, gravely,
watching me watching them.
The sun's arcing lower now.
It's 7 a.m. in September.
I'm washing blueberries
for pancakes.
Under the stove, a cricket
keeps time. At night
I watch the stars
and never get lonely.
My man's asleep in the loft,
back from the city.
He wants to still his mind.
After he came home,
I couldn't stop swallowing,
the way the Tao master
says a woman does
when she's ready for her man
to come into her.

SHE SHOULD HAVE GONE TO HIS ROOM

should have let flesh hold sway,
jettisoned the brittle weight of words,
plumbed the depths of her greed,
let the plunge and sob of bodies
unloose a knowing, beyond
the mirror-smooth beauty of reason.

GETTING LOST

I wake from sleep and sex,
and the show last night,
the encore we all sang:
>   Oh, give me the beat, boys,
>   and free my soul.
And the part about drifting away.
We sang it trailing off like clouds:
>   I wanna get lost
>   in your rock 'n' roll
>   and drift away.
"The chorus is profound,"
the singer said, "just 'cause it's popular
don't mean it ain't profound." Like sex,
I think—sex and a song—
always racing the loneliness
that drags us back,
however we drift away.

On Reading Jack Gilbert's "Bring in the Gods"

The man stands so as to see again
olive leaves above stone walls,
the wind, the bare breasts, the whimpers
of the women he'd loved,
not to label them *youth* or *past*
but to refuse to abandon
high heels in a furrowed field,
Perugia, ghosts in alleys of stone,
Lindos, the cities and the seas,
the taking of another into his hands,
the dazzle of it, the unforgotten giving.
He shoulders the weight of absence,
names it beautiful,
wields, under a northern sun,
a knowing,
a long blade
thinned, almost to light.

LETTERS TO CLINT EASTWOOD

*I don't think he cares now
how people see him.*
                Meryl Streep

i

You pan through our lives
like a miner searching for gold,
stirring up the meanness,
the stench and the fear,
sifting down to layers
long buried.
Sick to death of waste,
you pick from the muck,
love, muddied and abandoned,
to show us, how it falls like light,
unafraid of our violence,
our timidity, our hate.
Look! you say, *love glitters.*

ii

Pelted by the rain, you stand
in that time-forgotten Iowa town,
your halo of hair now lank and streaming,
your self erased
down to agony's ancient face,
and you really don't care
because, at last, something is important.
You, all those years groped toward that face,
peeling back layers of custom

and rectitude, even of beauty,
tunneling toward some absolute
you wanted badly, the way
you want those crosses in your movies.
You tuck them away in tattoos,
on rear view mirrors, and chapel walls
backlighting unlikely martyrs,
hide them where only
someone who needs them as much
will find them: love going one way,
agony the other, the crux
where they always meet,
where, whoever crosses there,
must let fall
whatever he has to hide.

AND THE GHOSTS COME DOWN

The sun polishes the bald heads
of Raymond and Mitchell,
warms the paunches
of their middle-aged friends
who gather in the marsh
to laugh too much but lovingly.
No mothers or fathers,
no sisters or brothers
attend the lovers,
but Tim says he's the flower boy,
and Trevor mans the camcorder, as someone
carries the rings to the minister
who asks Ray and Mitch *to have and to hold.*
The green marsh bows its strong grasses
toward them as Mitch promises Ray
he will always be his one,
and Raymond vows, "Mitch, I will be there
for you." Now the minister hands them to drink
the sweet and bitter wine of life, and tells them:
You are in the presence of the spirit.

And that's when the ghosts come down:
the once bewildered mothers,
the grandmas and grandpas
to whom no one listened, even the fathers
who wept in night's silences.
Shimmering and trembling,
the marsh's blue mirror
circles even the ghosts,
patting and chuckling now, teary,
like any wedding guests.

About Love

How, in its insistence,
its tentacled reach,
it sweeps clean
even the floor of self,
leaving such lovers to lie,
alone or together, no matter,
with the calm
of boulders beside the sea,
in blamelessness and solitude,
though weary perhaps,
a bit undone
as the old explorers were—
awed, almost disbelieving.

BODIES

All my members felt His in full felicity.
I wholly melted away in Him.

                    Hadewijch of Brabant

Even the solitary mystic—
it was her body God came to.
Love knows no abstractions.
It licks and sucks,
wounds and devours.
Even the infant stiff with desire,
tensing and mewling, roots
in tumescent flesh, hungry
as the mystics
for bliss,
that pure white milk.

PITTSBURGH SUNBATH

In winter window sun
my mother laid her newest baby girl.
I watched my sister
while my mother came and went,
chanting: *So she doesn't roll off,
so her bones will be straight.*
My sister kicked and waved
her fat-creased legs and arms.

I held my hands against the sun to see
those dark fish, my bones.
The morning sun is best, my mother
told me, but we took what came
in that city of crooked limbs
where light lingered
for just a moment.

My mother's black hair glistened,
her beauty bowed above
her baby's shell-pink flesh.
My hands in gloves of light
guarded our makeshift altar,
our prayer to fend off crookedness,
the dark god waiting within
to bend my sister's bones.

Three Vietnamese Girls Walk to School Carrying Umbrellas of Many Colors

    Small girls
wearing halos of rain-drinking flowers
on morning-empty Irving Street,
you tiptoe far
from mango-green rivers
and wail of monsoon.

    You place your white tennis shoes
in phosphorescent puddles,
first one toe, then another,
the way the white crane,
canopied by rain and flower,
enters the lagoon.

THE SILENCE

Between 1831 and 1916, the Boston Pilot
*published advertisements for thousands of
missing Irish immigrant women.*
                        from The Missing Friends Project

Sean O'Halloran's niece went missing
when her ship, without warning,
put in at Nova Scotia.
She stood tall, he advertised,
with black eyes and hair.

Had the nameless niece
met a Nova Scotian farmer
and, fearful of her family's anger,
promised herself she'd write next Christmas
or after she repaid her uncle
his steerage money?

Or with the island fog
blotting out even the shapes of the houses
and the farmer's baby kicking,
did everything seem a little hazy
as she searched in vain
for her uncle's address?

Or could the niece's dark eyes
have hidden an untrue heart?
Did the family where she took service
pride itself on a handsome son
who, she felt sure, wouldn't be wanting

to waste his money bringing over the others
who'd stomped tearfully on the pier
while she'd stood, dry-eyed and glad,
on the deck above them.

So, from the missing
a great silence arose,
whether because of fear
or muddle or greed,
or, perhaps, because one life
slid slowly over the other,
the way cities pile upon each other,
so that, in the end,
writing home would have been
as if sending a letter to ghosts:
You weren't sure
they would hear you
or if they even existed.

Immigrant Daughter's Song

Gone, the silver-green silk of time
winding down centuries
of custom and kinship,
the pouring of the sea, the stars
on the slate of night, the moon
stamping the spire of the church
on the sand. Time itself changed
to a ticking, a dot on a line.
Customs of grace
and gentleness gone
name-saying and knowing
who begat whom
and when and where
and who could work
and who could sing
and who would pray
and who would not
and where the fish ran
and the wild plums hid
and how the old mothers
fit babies' hands
to the five-flowered hollows
of blue ladyfingers,
and whose father fought whose
with golden swords
a thousand years ago
at Ballyferriter
on the strand below the church.
Gone from a silken spool unwinding

to rooms of relics and loss
behind whose locked doors
I dream, not daring to wake.

THE HOUSE ON BROUGHTON STREET

Always it was a summer afternoon.
I see my mother climbing the stairs
to the porch,
my grandmother waiting,
tiny but formidable.
She'd been expecting her,
the sisters smiling
brothers watching.
My mother in her grey crepe,
the white gloves she always wore.
Her hair and eyes dark
among these fair freckled people.
My father shyly presenting her,
something of his own.
Shuffling, they made room for her
and she took her place among them
and between them
grew something new.
Marie, they came to say,
this is Grant's Marie.
She seldom spoke
but rested among them,
a harbor she'd found.

My father gave her a carnelian ring,
the stone surrounded by silver hearts.
Before Grandma died
she gave my mother
the diamond brooch from Grandpa.

My mother brought with her
fabrics that glistened,
a wrap of velvet,
sometimes a feather.
They noticed the light
in the rooms where she sat.
And even thirty years later
after the lost jobs and the babies,
after the mortgages and the wars,
what they remembered most
was the way my mother
set aside her gloves.

She was buried on Good Friday.
There was a blizzard.
After the funeral
the youngest uncle
read *Murder in the Cathedral* aloud.
I have the carnelian ring now,
the diamond brooch.
I wear satin when I can
and I am attracted to old houses
where the light passes
across the porch to the windows, making
of the space between a grace.

BLOOD LINES

i

Great-grandfather Grant banishes
his eldest from the house. The boy
refuses to pray.
Great-grandfather Connors, mad for gold,
turns his back, heads West.
And somewhere his tall son
captures the sober gaze
of Michael Grant's small daughter.
Their shy boy wins Marie,
Grandma's Lily's dark-eyed girl,
and I am born of Grant and Marie.

ii

I want to know what's inside
a seed, a radio, my sister's skin.
I never smile. My father
complains. I stay small and wait,
catch fireflies, stomp open buckeyes,
look for what glitters, what can be
caught and uncovered. I love my mother
dumbly, completely. Marie longs
for robins and lilacs. I think about fairies
and God. I swallow Jesus, careful
he does not stick to the roof of my mouth.
On All Souls' Day I rescue the sinners
in Purgatory, running in and out
of the church of Our Lady.
I pray, Michael Grant, I pray. I never

think of money, Great-grandfather Connors,
I never think of money.

iii

Blood and breasts. The vault
of Our Lady's church holds me
smaller than a buckeye.
I don't know where God lives.
Candles flicker like fireflies.
It is Lent. A dark hollow
blows open within me. Love arrives,
scary and delicious. My body
tells me what to do. My mother
grows small, a burning wick
upon the altar of Our Lady,
and goes out.

iv

Only my babies wake me.
I take them to the priest.
He promises me: *Eternal life*,
he says, *eternal life*. My mother
speaks to me from lilacs. I remember
what to do: I pray,
never think of money,
call back the ancestors.
I say their names:
Michael Grant, Lily,
Great-grandfather Connors,
the banished uncle,
Marie and Grant.
I say their names.

Too Much

Grandma, why is the door locked?
We're hungry. We want pancakes.

You speak with the indignation,
the disbelief of the always loved,
who've glimpsed in the muddle
of a locked door, in the shock
of absence—an ending
like the coyote's howl fading away.
Love a mirage after all.

I don't tell you
that what you fear is real,
or that I know little of love—
not how to tame it
to curl by the fire—
only that I cling to it,
no matter how tenuous
and, knowing this,
make you pancakes each morning.

Nor do I tell you
of the world's randomness,
its starry indifference
or how small and rare and
forgetful we are.
I light the fire,
flip the pancakes,
heat the syrup
and pour, on each plate,
too much.

NEIGHBORS

I have nothing to give Mrs. Danley.
I have no babies she cannot carry,
no plants she's too feeble to water,
no food she cannot eat.
I have nothing Mrs. Danley needs.

I cannot bring her the island
she cruised to in pink chiffon,
the gallant captain bent low over her hand,
nor her father, struck crossing the road
his first night up from Mississippi,

nor Andre of the luminous eyes,
gunned down in his prom tuxedo.
Nor can I make the girl she once was,
beautiful and beloved,
walk out of the heart-shaped frame

to take Mrs. Danley
in strong arms and exclaim:
"I never expected to see
anything so beautiful today,"

which is how my neighbor,
waiting in red velvet, greets me
as I step empty-handed
through her open door.

LAS MADRES DE PLAZA DE MAYO

In a silence strong as water,
Las Madres de Plaza hold aloft
photos of their children
for all to see, the way
mothers do at parties.
What could be more natural?
Juan Pablo Ramirez, age 22,
missing 6-11-77;
Ada Estabar, age 17,
missing 2-10-79.
Pedro, Estela, Salvador.

These mothers have coupled with death
and nothing prevails against them,
not the years, the evil
of their own kind, nor the memories,
waiting always to dissolve them,
of those tender unshriven bodies.
Birthing a huge implacable animal,
Las Madres de Plaza de Mayo
circle the square.

GOING SOMEWHERE

Has anyone written of Pauline,
that tiny tank of a nurse,
the one who sat behind Eddie
in third grade,
the one with the silky pigtails
who couldn't spell,
the one he lost track of
when they both lost track
of whatever it was
they were supposed to remember.

Has anyone told,
after fifty years drifted by
the slow way the morning fog
lifts off the pond,
how Pauline barreled into Eddie's room,
to pull up the blinds,
and shoo away the dust
that comes with dying,
to make him a bed of snowy sheets.
And, though he protested weakly,
to wash him clean, and say
she wasn't going anywhere.

And when, with all her doing,
she could not stop his trembling
and his fear,
has it been set down anywhere
how Pauline climbed

into Eddie's clean-sheeted bed
to hold close
in her strong plump arms
his beautiful head,
his slack-skinned flesh,
to rock him on out
as far as she could go,
beyond third grade
and the lives they lived
and the lives they hadn't lived
and the ones they wished
they hadn't lived.

Has anyone told,
does anyone know,
what kind of love that is?

DEATH WATCH

i.m. Barbara Angell

I match my voice to yours.
You lead a song
I might spoil
with a false note.

Like having my first baby, you say,
I don't know if I can do it.
I count the spaces between your breaths
as decades ago someone counted
the seconds between your pains.

DEATH OF A FRIEND

Toward the end we talked fast
as though the brown shirts
were rushing at the door,
but I always went away thinking
I was forgetting to tell you
the most important thing.

We were never big on talking anyway.
Mostly we looked
at waves and morning skies
and wallpaper books,
at light and mist and paintings.
And we walked. We walked
in the sun and the rain,
on beaches, in woods, over the twine fields.
And we breathed
with the water and the dunes and the trees
marching along, looking and looking.
And the only thing you ever did wrong
was bring sand into the bedrooms.
And the only thing I ever did wrong
was that once someone gave me a Waldorf cake
and I couldn't remember what it looked like.
You'd sigh and wonder about the cake
while I'd sweep sand down the stairs.
And I made my poems
and you painted your water lilies,
and all this went on for years,

which is why, at the end,
I could never remember
what was most important to say.

So I'd put ice on your arm
and you'd tell me *I'm so blessed*
and we'd doze, and finally,
in the mustard-green silence
of a July afternoon
they came and took you.

CERTAIN THINGS

The worst of it is
I'll never be able to tell you
certain things. For example,
that Yeats had a brother
whose watercolors
have the same break-your-heart music
as Yeats' poetry,
and Charles, knowing this,
began the Irish book
with a watercolor the brother made
of Innisfree. It says all there is to say
about Ireland, down to its tenuousness.
You know, that wavery feeling
made of water and light.

And in the Sunday paper a photo
of Paul Newman and Joanne Woodward
as a Midwestern middle-aged couple,
maybe in the late 20's,
right before the Depression.
It was fall.
She had an airborne quality to her,
one hand up to the brim of her felt hat.
He stood planted like a tree,
thumbs hooked in his vest pockets,
a gold watch chain glittering between.
But what I wanted to tell you
was about the way she held her hand
in the crook of his arm, the way
it lightly rested there,

the way her hand became a part of him
the way his arm belonged to her.

This morning on the white sunporch
the light was so brilliant
when I awoke
that for just a second
I floated weightless.
I remembered your saying
a few days before you died:
We each have a shimmering
that goes with us.

A KIND OF VICTORY

Walking at Head of the Meadow,
I try to wrap my mind around the water
like Thoreau did, but when I can't,
I get that exact defeated feeling
I got with your death: I mean
death and the ocean give no quarter,
yet one can't deny they're beautiful.
Beauty's easy to see
in those seal-back swells
wheeling to marbled swirls,
but your dying was beautiful too,
no matter the mess
and the pain and the smells.
Something about the way,
even though you were scared
and truly had no use for death—
slinking somewhere between
the day lilies and the picture of Jesus
the church lady pinned to your wall—
you still didn't say *why me* or
try to bargain or get mad.
You stood straight up to death
the way a wave stands up,
transparent
and, really, most beautiful then,
before it falls.

You Could Have Lived

I would show you
what I wrote this morning
about the nun
who beat poor John Daugherty.
"No one to touch her," you would say.
And I'd be pleased to speak with you
about such things once more,
perhaps hear you decide:
"Beauty can come out of anything."

While the tide lays bare the flats,
we would sit talking
for a long time.
You might remember that day, when,
line and color not enough,
you put down your paints for poetry.
"Like going through a wall,"
you'd tell me again.

The slanted sun on our feet
would remind us of Li Ho:
how a purple man
driving a red dragon
was sent to honor Li Ho, who, dying,
had thought his poems forgotten.
How Li Ho wept.
We'd be quiet awhile
glad about the red dragon.
We would say: "How still the bay tonight,
how far our voices carry."

SPIRALING

A benign yellow school bus
chugs up my road and, suddenly,
John Daugherty's long-ago screams
spiral again from my fourth grade cloakroom.
We sit teacherless, still, eyes guarded
in a silence that deepens
as Sister pushes John
back into the room—her red face,
his wet one—and how we stare,
as though at a movie,
as he stumbles back to his seat.

Now I think of the young untouched nun
and wonder who shook her past pity
for John's smudged papers,
his unfocused eyes,
and if she prayed that night
and, if so, for forgiveness, or
did she feel cleansed, the way we do
when anger twists us in its teeth
to leave us limp and empty.

Mrs. Daugherty came the next day
in a too-long winter coat,
odd, with injured brown eyes.
We were surprised, perhaps
that John had a mother,
perhaps at love.
We had a book about the saints.
One of them was always
"cloaked in sorrow."

After You Died

i.m. Gillian Rudd

I'd heard that the soul
hovers near the body awhile
before beginning its journey,
so I drove through the night city
past the black river
to sit by your bed.
And I remembered how
in the old books, the women
washed and anointed the bodies
of those they'd loved
but, mostly, I had some animal urge
to go to you, not to leave you
alone in your trouble.
Though I had no myrrh
nor white linen to wrap you in,
I rubbed lotion on your tired hands
and wound through your fingers
a white rose and some baby's breath
from the windowsill bouquet.
Your nails red and perfect
as always.

A wet night, no moon or stars
above the invisible trees.
The nurse came in and out.
We talked. She was good.
I'm glad you had a good nurse
the night you died.

As your skin grew cool,
I wondered if your soul was passing,
while I sat there beside you
just hanging out the way we did
even that first month we met,
pulling grass from between the bricks
in my courtyard, happy and quiet,
talking on and on, two girls
with plenty of life left to live.

WHAT SHE WANTED

Waters, brisk waters, cover
her now, pull her
under your wavery scrim.
Unwind her fallow limbs
to float, stippled
in watery sun. In her hair,
tangle hermits and stars.
For them, planet, earth,
home she'll be, her skin
no longer skin, but
rolling sea-loam now
where light's flowers
dissolve and bloom.

BLUEFISH IN SEPTEMBER

Silver-scaled and slippery
in the blue-milk
sometime-pewter light,
you swivel your body
like I never can.

And I want you,
your quickness,
the way you don't care
or scheme or boast
of your weightless blue happiness.

Catch me.
I want to jettison thought.
I want to be blue
unknowing
coveted.

My Life's a Speck on a Horizon
I Can't Get To

My life didn't want
lists and parties and houses.
It was greedy for a rhythm
like the drum of a pulsing heart,
or maybe a silence,
the one the stars poke through.
My life begged me to live it,
not to be sad and worn, but juicy
like a red-headed girl turned thirteen
whose silhouette bounces
on a drawn green shade.
What my life wanted danced that way,
not frightened and skittery,
not worried about pills and money.
So I don't blame my life for going.
I want everyone to know that.
I would've gone too
if my mother hadn't taught me
to finish my dusting first,
and if everyone's hearts
didn't forever need mending,
and if I weren't scared
that when I got there
my life might be only an echo
I'd once heard.

A SMALL LIFE

I wake thinking of Henry Mitchell,
Miss Arabella's brother, my neighbor
across the alley. How he wouldn't shake my hand
when we first met. Later, he no longer hid
from me the stumps of his missing fingers,
the knotted scars. And a decade later still,
how he painted the kids' graffiti
from our alley wall, brush in one hand,
oxygen tank in the other, apologizing
because the color was a little off.
How in the good years between,
his ladies came and went, their voices
music in the hush of summer mornings:
I'll call you, Henry.

A small man with corn rows, a big TV,
and a house of his own, but
so sick after Miss Arabella died,
he opened his door only a crack
to take the ham for her funeral
down in the Tidewater
where their people came from.
Why do I wake feeling
that something's not been given
to Henry Mitchell—like the blanket
I once rattled my crib for,
crying for what was mine.

THE EXCHANGE

Graves said soldiers knew
they were soon to die
when they were struck
by the world's beauty.
They must have felt
they'd lived a lifetime,
vanities of self all vanishing,
as they exchanged themselves
for a world undiluted by greed
or desire. Perhaps their souls
grew content as the world in pity
lifted its veil, as they took
deep into themselves
the wild insistent loveliness
of passing time.

Even Small Things

i.m. Bill Cole

I took the mockingbird to the vet,
I told you, so my weeping nine-year-old
would know that this bird she'd nursed
was more important than spelling tests
and times tables, and her love more valuable
than the vet's small fee. But that $10 charge
enraged you. You saw it as one more strand
in a web the world spins
to toy with the good and the helpless:
Japan after the war, the flames of Beirut,
your own Arkansas—years of witnessing
massed behind your rage, exploding
over the bird's almost invisible
grey-brown tremors. That night,
after we'd buried the bird
and my daughter slept,
you told me, clutching your vodka,
how in a Moscow bar
you'd sat mesmerized
by a young pianist
until a militiaman, grinning,
slammed the piano lid down
on his unsuspecting fingers.

TIDES

Some say there's a sound
when the tide turns.
I say silence—
          long muscle of water
wrestled back, harboring vestigial sense
of an earth once flooded and subdued.
Power unspent
and no appeal.

Silence, the only course
when penned and bound.
Dignity demands it.
          Kazantzakis' wife railed
at their captors. The poet
stood mute, his only answer
to brute force: silence.
And grace, that quiet turn.

GOD ON THE PLAINS

Sometimes they felt, above them,
the sole of His boot, their smallness.
Faith a shawl they huddled under,
giving Him their grain,
their calves, their children. *Thy will,*
Thy will, they muttered
and they praised Him,
blessed Him,
could not let Him go.
They bowed their heads
and bent their backs,
beseeched Him with fork and spade.
What had they left undone?
Of their guilt they were certain,
yet He would spare them,
cosset them again
in the palm of His hand,
ragged as they were
and hard to love—
blistered and parched.

Surely His grace, beyond
the reach of even the diviner's rod,
must be like water
free of salt's sting.
It would stream over them, over
the cracked earth. His fruits
would come forth, and to His rain
they would lift their leather faces,
smooth again, and pure,

as they'd once been,
before He unloosed
His clenched fist
and scattered them,
like seeds, or locusts,
across the plains.

FARMER PLOWING

after a painting by Ross Moffett

Moffett did it all in curves.
The horses' ribs billow
on a great breath,
stomachs curl to rumps,
the farmer's back bows
to his bent arm,
even his red suspenders flow.
And, of course, the ribbony furrows
turn and turn beneath
the hills humming
like a fugue
under cumulus clouds.
Even the tongue
of the bony white dog
circled small in the corner
coils to the fleas
at the base of his poised tail,
naming us kin:
cloud hill farmer
horse dog flea.

A Flower Girl Confesses

I do still miss you, God,
(and my cloud of a veil
with its rosebuds of ribbons,
our white dresses and the processions
where we scattered roses
and peonies, moist and dripping
from the church ladies' gardens)
though I never told you
I loved your mother best.

You were all weathers, God,
forgive me, even a little unreliable,
preoccupied. You had a job to do,
certain that blood and thorns
could save us. But it was Mary
did the godly work—cradled
your pitiful body in her arms
and washed you clean.

And isn't that what saves us?
Someone to hold us
at the end, no matter
how bloody or crazy
we've been.

MIRAGE

*...I read and write and try
to dream her back again....*
Linda Gregg

She dons a long white gown,
drifts over a mountain
to a hut high in a meadow.
The hem of her dress brushes poppies.
Her footprints leave no trace.
Her sash is blue
and trails a long way behind her.
In the snow she carries roses.
We follow her. Our hearts
make the sound of a small gray bird
scratching against glass.
Her hair flames golden or red or
glitters like a crow's wing.
Sometimes she rests under a tree
by a brook, listens
to water on stone—
the way they are opposite
and love one another.

WAITING FOR THE MUSE

> *...I desired above all things to know*
> *Sister of the mirage and echo.*
>> from the dedication to
>> *The White Goddess,*
>> by Robert Graves

The poet sits in his easy chair,
hope vanishing
like the steam from his chipped mug.
He's waiting for his blue-eyed girl,
the one with the honey-colored hair.
The clock ticks.
She'll stop it
when she comes. And she will come,
except—there's always a last time,
and the tart will never tell him: *This is it*
or *good-bye.* She's all good news,
all shimmer and glow, her voice
bubbling on and on, until
he's young again, caught up
in the threads of her hair
which he follows
into the maze of himself,
to the place where only she
knows the turns—the last time
as good as the first.

STARS AT 4 A.M. IN LATE AUGUST

In a great hush
just right for a god,
Jupiter rises,
Orion and the twins
prostrate above him.
Procyon, unfettered, erect,
tempers the frivolous Pleiades.
Though teased by the horns of the Bull,
they dance only in place,
as Sirius, bold dazzler, promenades
to the feet of the god.
For this entourage,
no cacophony of drums or bugle blare,
just a silence made visible,
in the measured ascension,
the mad revolution of light.

THINGS

All things wait,
humble and profound,
in the stillness of matter,
in the lushness
of being.
    Their patience
old as starlight
huddled and pooled, content
in what they are:
wood forever thirsty,
spade and spoon
and your grandfather's quilt—
their dents and scratches and tears.
All contained in a long solitude,
in the mute eloquence of themselves.
    Unknowable, no matter
the dark boulder
of our desire, no matter
the blue-milk light
of their yearning.

I TALK TO GOD

Remember that Ohio glass factory town,
the drafty church where I finally realized
You were me?
You'd already taught me
what a God must do.
Forgiveness takes the most work. No,
even harder is doing without You,
or, maybe remembering I'm glorious.
Yes, that's the hardest part.
It's one thing to be glorious
with angels and trumpets and clouds.
But try bosses and TV and sleet?
And I don't need to tell You,
it's lonely. You never told me
what the leaves and the animals,
the stars showed me—

that I was a god
who would die.
Nobody holds me now
in the palm of His hand.
I have only myself to pray to.
Sometimes I'm tempted
to float You back to Your cloud,
Your long white beard
winding me in forgiveness,
but then I see that winter church,
those plaster of Paris statues
their pea-green robes—
those vacant painted eyes.

THAT DEEP AND STEADY HUM

The Catholics take such good care
of the church of Our Lady.
Last Monday just after dawn,
with furrowed brow, the sign man
gilded again the letters of her name.
Each week the tiny white-haired woman
carries in the linens,
old but crisp and snowy white,
while the hedge man cuts
the hedges straight as truth.
Familiar and awe-struck as lovers
all of them, even the young artist
who ran amuck that winter night,
his blue eyes empty and unseeing,
and took an ax to the icons of Our Lady.

He came in the dark
with his unsuckled rage,
his sweet blank face,
carrying the ax
the way the old woman
held the linens,
she to adorn,
he, the one with the golden curls,
to destroy.
And when at last
someone took the ax
and led him away,
his lightning anger
dimming into blankness,

shards of her icons
painted by long-ago hands
lay splintered on the floor,
along with his rage,
and he wept.

What did he know
of great and quiet care,
of love pure as milk,
of forgiveness hungry to forgive:
that deep and steady hum
girdling oceans and moons
and the tiny shrines
we care for and destroy.

PROCYON

They call you Little Dog,
but you dazzled me
that midnight in October—
the uprightness of
you,
saluting me.

No lolling on your back
like Orion and the Twins,
or the Pleiades,
appearing and vanishing
in an agony of indecision.
Nor like Big Dog,
with his entourage
and stud collar,
tail cocked
and running.

I held my breath
that October night
and straightened up,
the way a soldier might
when a general he loves
shows him
who he could be.

ORION

You beam down courage
raise your club, dangle
your sword and don't care.
Sometimes I think
you're asleep up there:
Betelgeuse twitching in a red dream,
Rigel stirring to stomp
on our cowardice, our smallness,
the way we don't shine
with your insouciant glitter. Your belt's
the only sop to order except, of course,
the great sprawling faithfulness of you.

It's 4 A.M. in September 2000.
I'm crouched on the loft's white steps
like the hare at your feet,
timid and cold, and I need to know:
Did we throw you above us
to mirror the light
forgotten in our fractured hearts?

THE WOMEN TALK ABOUT THE RAIN

Did you hear the rain last night?
> *Mmm, it came so fast,*
> *such a pounding. You heard it?*
Yes, it woke me. I didn't
want it to end, did you? Did you
want it to end?
> *No, I didn't. I wanted*
> *it to go on forever.*
I did too. The heavens
just opened, didn't they?
> *Yes, and the rain poured down.*
> *You heard the pounding?*
Yes, yes, I heard it. It spilled down,
thundered down, though
there was no thunder.
> *No, just the rain*
> *coming so fast, ferociously*
> *it seemed.*
Yes, so heavy. The clouds
swollen. Everything
trembling.
> *Oh, it was wild. No question,*
> *the weight of it. I felt flattened.*
Yes, I held my breath
for fear it would stop. Did you?
Did you hold your breath?
> *Oh, I did. And I shut my eyes.*
> *I just wanted it*
> *not to stop. Did you want that?*
Yes, of course, I wanted that but

it did stop.

> *It did. It didn't last. Not long
> enough, not really.*

No, not long enough.
Not nearly.

WHAT SHE LOVED

i.m. Rachel Carson

The ocean's long snow of seed
and sediment, shell and skeleton—
limy and silicious—
the flecks of husk and weed,
castoffs of mountain drivel,
river ooze. The sea's purchase,
its constancy. The calm and unrelenting
diminution of matter:
the diatom's unseen shells,
what the floods took and released,
skimmings of desert winds,
tooth of whale and the bone's shearings,
the glacier's blue bounty
lost in the hair of clouds,
all endlessly arriving.

Nothing refused
of these fragile chroniclers:
silt and melt and meteors,
the irresistible flakes
of the soft radiolarians,
the whispery mollusks
once plump with light.
These possessed her,
not the sea's high billows, the crest,
the depths where color's lost,
the trough that toys with ship and gull.
Not these, but what was worn

and unwanted—earth's detritus,
the sea's snow, flake by flake
falling through a watery patience
salvaging time's story.

NOTES

"Angell's Toenails" (page 3): Hendrick van Loon, *The Story of Mankind*.

"Once, You Will Say" (page 6): *Zanjero* is Spanish for "ditch rider." The *zanjeros* operate the canal and ditch gates in the vast irrigation system of the Southwest.

"Certainty" (page 12): This incident is taken from Beatrice's testimony before the Inquisition as recounted in *Montaillou* by Emmanuel Le Roy Ladurie.

"Getting Lost" (page 19): Mentor Williams' song was sung by Steve Young.

"You Could Have Lived" (page 47): The story of Li Ho is found in Charles Wright's "Poem Half in the Manner of Li Ho" in Wright's book *Black Zodiac*.

"The Exchange" (page 55): Robert Graves, *Good-Bye to All That*.

"Tides" (page 57): Nikos Kazantzakis, the Greek novelist, and his wife were imprisoned by the Germans on Crete during World War II.

"Farmer Plowing" (page 60): Ross Moffett painted primarily in Provincetown in the early and mid-1900's.

"What She Loved" (page 73): Rachel Carson, *The Sea Around Us*.

Acknowledgments

Grateful acknowledgment is made to the editors and publishers of the following publications in which these poems appeared, some of them in a slightly different form. I am particularly grateful to the publishers of my now out-of-print chapbooks in which some of these poems appeared: *The Coil of the Skin* (Washington Writers' Publishing House), *A Shimmering That Goes With Us* (Finishing Line Press) and *gods and flesh* (Plan B Press). I am also grateful to the members of the Big Mama Poetry Troupe and the Capitol Hill Poetry Group, particularly Meredith Holmes, Jean Nordhaus, Shirley Cochrane and Patric Pepper, who have long shared in the life of the imagination with me. Special thanks go to the Jentel Foundation for quiet time in Wyoming, and to Barry Sternlieb who meticulously and intuitively read this particular manuscript.

The Baltimore Review: "Three Vietnamese Girls Walk to School Carrying Umbrellas of Many Colors"

Beltway and *Plainsongs:* "Farmer Plowing"

Fathers and Children and *Ireland in Poetry*, Harry N. Abrams; *The Irish*, Hugh Lauter Levin Associates; and *The Irish Americans*, McDougal Littell, a Houghton Mifflin Company: "Immigrant Daughter's Song"

Potato Eyes: "Death Watch"

Free Lunch: "Bluefish in September"

The Innisfree Poetry Journal: "Waiting for the Muse"

In the West of Ireland, Enright House: "This Is a Song"

The Lover's Companion, Harry N. Abrams: "Keeping Time"

Meridians: "Neighbors"

Mobius: "Stars at 4 A.M. in Late August"

New Letters and *Voices of Cleveland*, Cleveland State University Poetry Center: "Certain Things"

Out of Line: "Las Madres de Plaza de Mayo"

The Other Side of the Hill, Forest Woods Media Productions: "After You Died," "That Deep and Steady Hum"

Poetry Greece: "Once, You Will Say," "Death of a Friend"

Poet Lore: "Orion"

Poetry Ireland Review: "The Exchange"

WPFW Anthology, The Bunny and Crocodile Press, and *The Strip:* "Pittsburgh Sunbath"

ABOUT THE AUTHOR

Mary Ann Larkin is author of five chapbooks of poetry:
The Coil of the Skin, White Clapboard (with A. Brockie
Stevenson), *The DNA of the Heart* (with her husband
Patric Pepper), *A Shimmering That Goes With Us* and *gods
& flesh*. Her poetry has appeared in numerous magazines
such as *Poetry Ireland Review, New Letters* and *Poetry Greece*
and in a score of anthologies, including *America in Poetry*
and *Ireland in Poetry*, the art and poetry series published
by Harry N. Abrams. In the seventies in Cleveland, Ohio,
she co-founded the Big Mama Poetry Troupe, a group
of feminist poets who performed from Chicago to New
York. She has earned her living as a writer, fundraiser
and teacher, most recently at Howard University. With
Patric Pepper she co-founded Pond Road Press whose
latest publication is *Tough Heaven: Poems of Pittsburgh* by
Jack Gilbert. Born in Pittsburgh, Pennsylvania, she lives
in Washington, D.C. and North Truro, Massachusetts.

CPSIA information can be obtained at www.ICGtesting.com
Printed in the USA
BVOW011656131111

275927BV00002B/13/P